HAL•LEONARD ESSENTIAL SONGS

PIANO VOCAL GUITAR

The 2000s

D0898501

ISBN 0-634-09099-2

HAL•LEONARD® CORPORATION

7777 W. BLUEMOUND RD. P.O. BOX 13819 MILWAUKEE, WI 53213

Visit Hal Leonard Online at
www.halleonard.com

CONTENTS

200	If I'm Not Made for You (If You're Not the One)	Daniel Bedingfield	15	2003
206	In a Little While	Uncle Kracker	59	2002
212	Invisible	Clay Aiken	37	2004
218	Jenny from the Block	Jennifer Lopez featuring Jadakiss and Styles	3	2002
226	Lady Marmalade	Christina Aguilera, Lil' Kim, Mya & Pink	1	2001
236	Lucky	Britney Spears	23	2000
243	Meant to Live	Switchfoot	18	2004
250	A Moment Like This	Kelly Clarkson	1	2002
258	1985	Bowling for Soup	72	2004
274	On the Way Down	Ryan Cabrera	20	2004
280	100 Years	Five For Fighting	28	2004
290	Out of My Heart (Into Your Head)	BBMak	56	2002
296	Rain on Me	Ashanti	7	2003
302	Rock the Boat	Aaliyah	14	2001
310	She Bangs	Ricky Martin	12	2000
265	She Will Be Loved	Maroon5	9	2004
318	So Yesterday	Hilary Duff	42	2003
324	Somewhere Out There	Our Lady Peace	44	2002
336	The Space Between	Dave Matthews Band	22	2001
331	Take My Breath Away (Love Theme)	Jessica Simpson	20	2004
344	Thank You	Dido	3	2001
350	There You'll Be	Faith Hill	10	2001
355	This Love	Maroon5	5	2004
362	A Thousand Miles	Vanessa Carlton	5	2002
370	Underneath Your Clothes	Shakira	9	2002
375	Wasting My Time	Default	13	2002
382	Wherever You Will Go	The Calling	5	2002
394	Who Let the Dogs Out	Baha Men	40	2000
388	You Raise Me Up	Josh Groban	73	2004

ACCIDENTALLY IN LOVE
from the Motion Picture SHREK 2

Words and Music by
ADAM F. DURITZ

_____ will fol-low af-ter. Come on, come on, 'cause ev-'ry-bod-y's af-ter love. _____

So I said _____ I'm a

snow - ball run - ning, _____ run-ning down in-to the spring that's com-ing. All this _____

_____ love melt-ing un-der blue skies, belt-ing out sun-light, shim-mer-ing

ALL OR NOTHING

Words and Music by WAYNE HECTOR
and STEVE MAC

know when he's been on your mind, ___ the dis- tant look is in your eyes, ___ I
There are times it seems to me ___ I'm shar- ing you with mem- o- ries. ___ I

thought with time you'd re- al- ize, ___ it's o- ver, o- ver. It's not the way I chose to live, ___ and
feel it in my heart, but I ___ don't show it, show it. And then there's times you look at me ___ as

all, or noth - ing ___ at all. There's no - where left ___ to

fall when you reach the bot - tom; it's now or nev - er. Is it all, or are we ___ just

friends? ___ Is this how. it ends, with a sim - ple tel - e-phone call? You leave me here with noth - ing at

all, all.

ALWAYS

Lyrics by JOSEY SCOTT
Music by BOB MARLETTE and JOSEY SCOTT

I hear _ a voice say, "Don't be so blind." _ It's tell-ing me all these things _
I feel _ like you don't want me a - round. _ I guess I'll pack all my things.

that you would prob - ab - ly hide. Am I _ your one and on - ly de - sire?
I guess I'll see you a - round. It's all _ been bot - tled up un - til now.

_ Am I the rea - son you breathe, _ or am I the rea - son you cry? _ Al - ways,
_ As I walk out your door _ all _ I can hear is the sound _ of al - ways, } al - ways,

* Recorded a half step lower.

BEAUTIFUL

Words and Music by
LINDA PERRY

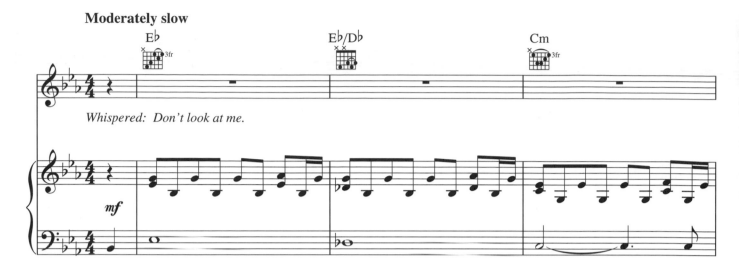

Whispered: Don't look at me.

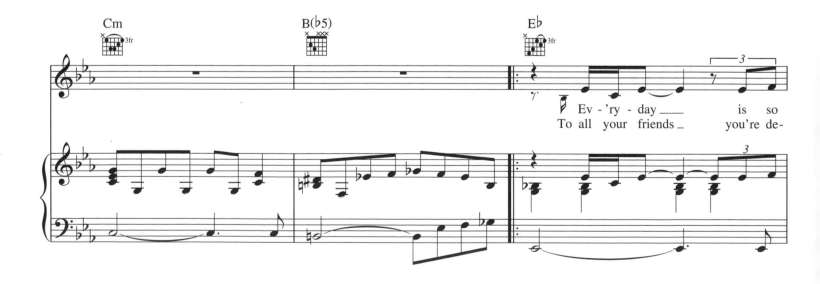

Ev - 'ry - day ___ is so
To all your friends ___ you're de-

So don't you _ bring me down to-day. _____ No mat-ter what _ we do. _

No mat-ter what _ we say. __ We're the song in-side _ the tune _

full of beau-ti-ful mis-takes. And ev-'ry-where _ we go _

the sun will al-ways shine. _ And to-mor-row we might a-wake _

BENT

Written by
ROB THOMAS

well, pick me up ___ and dust me off. ___

BLESSED

Words and Music by BRETT JAMES,
HILLARY LINDSEY and TROY VERGES

hear my chil - dren laugh - ing down the hall through the bed - room door.

Some-times I sit on my __ front porch __ swing, just

soak - in' up the day. _____ I think to my - self, I

think to my - self this world is a beau - ti - ful place. I have been

When I, when I'm sing-in' my

kids to sleep, ___ when I feel you hold-in' me, ___

CASE OF THE EX
(Whatcha Gonna Do)

Words and Music by CHRISTOPHER STEWART,
TRACI HALE and THABISO NKHEREANYE

It's af-ter mid-night _ and she's on _ your phone. She's
There's no _ need to rem-i-nisce 'bout _ the past,

say-ing _ come o-ver, 'cause she's all _ a-lone. I
ob-vi-ous-ly, 'cause _ that shit did _ not last. I

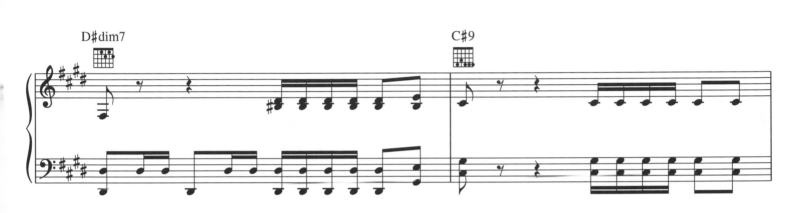

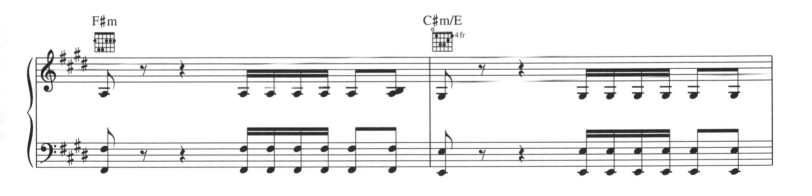

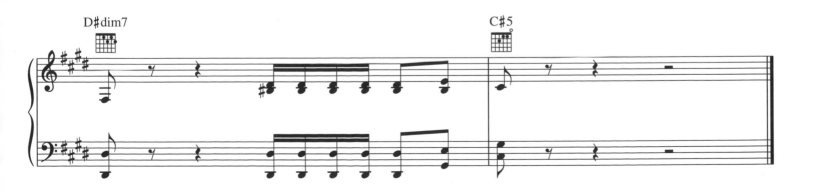

BREATHE

Words and Music by HOLLY LAMAR
and STEPHANIE BENTLEY

Moderately fast

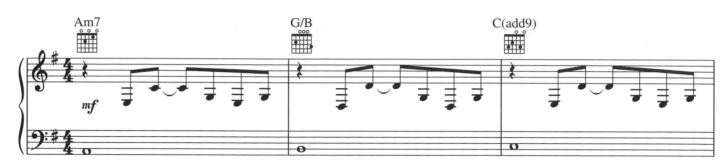

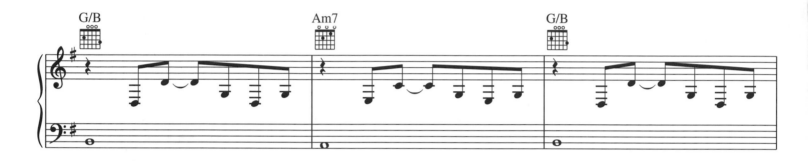

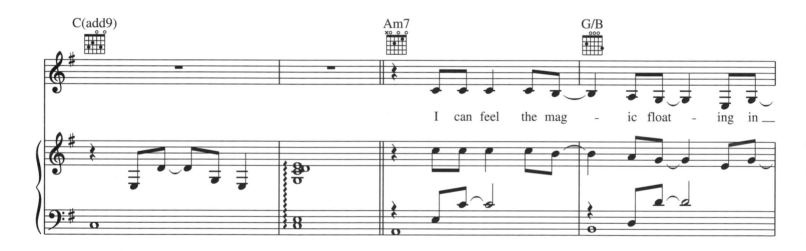

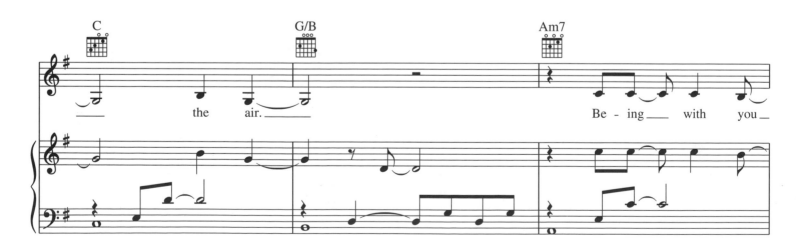

BREATHLESS

Words and Music by ROBERT LANGE,
ANDREA CORR, CAROLINE CORR,
JAMES CORR and SHARON CORR

Steady Dance beat

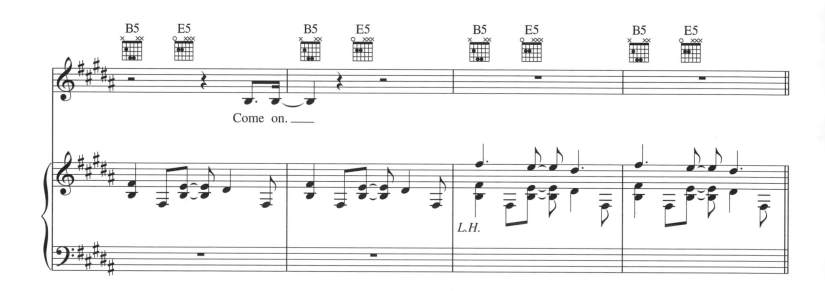

CALLING ALL ANGELS

Words and Music by PAT MONAHAN,
SCOTT UNDERWOOD, JAMES STAFFORD
and CHARLIE COLIN

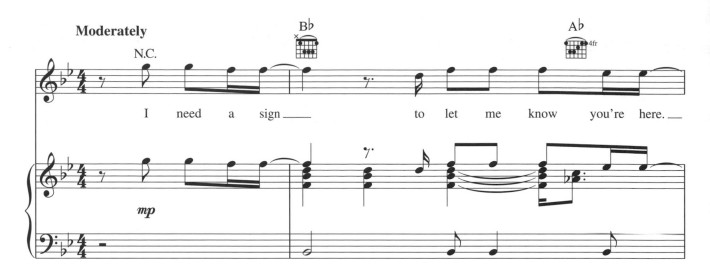

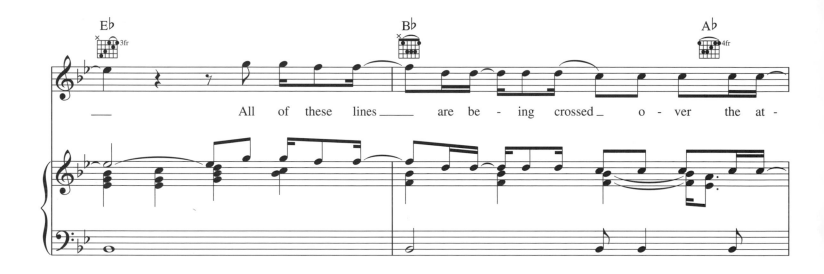

call - ing ___ all an - gels. ___

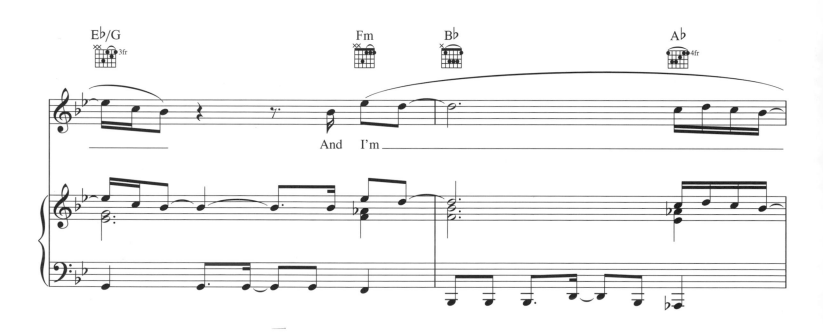

And I'm ___

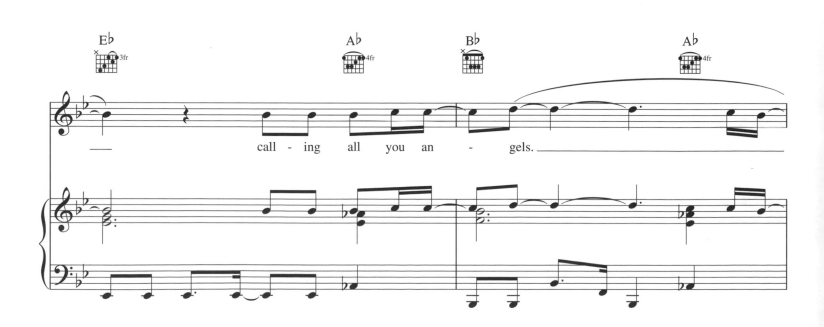

call - ing all you an - gels. ___

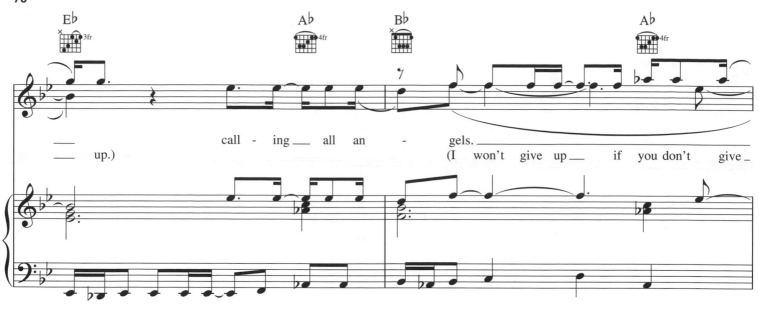

call - ing __ all an - gels. _____
__ up.)
(I won't give up __ if you don't give _

__ up.) __
And I'm _____
(I won't give up __ if you don't give _

call - ing all you an - gels. _____
__ up.)
(I won't give up __ if you don't give _

Repeat and Fade

Calling all you an - gels. ___ (I won't give up ___ if you don't give ___

___ up.)

Calling all you an - gels. ___ (I won't give up ___ if you don't give ___

___ up.)

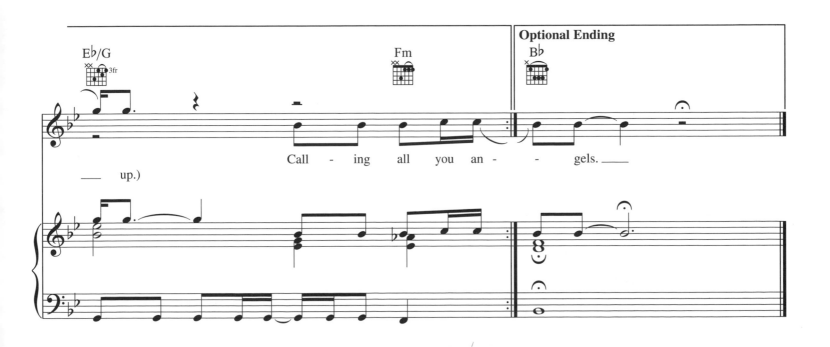

Optional Ending

Calling all you an - - gels. ___

___ up.)

CLOCKS

Words and Music by GUY BERRYMAN, JON BUCKLAND,
WILL CHAMPION and CHRIS MARTIN

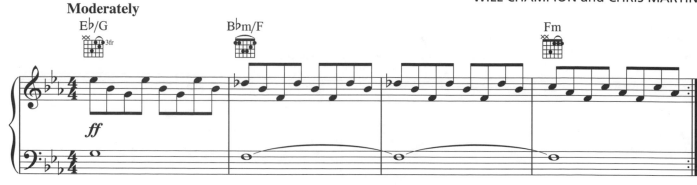

Lights go out and I can't be saved. ___ Tides that I tried to
Con - fu - sion ___ nev - er stops. ___ Clos - ing ___ walls and

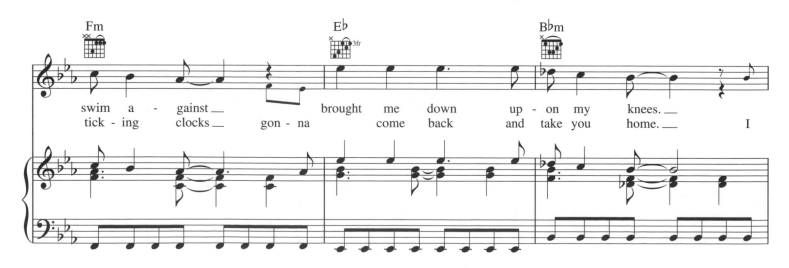

swim a - gainst ___ brought me down up - on my knees. ___
tick - ing clocks ___ gon - na come back and take you home. ___ I

And noth - ing else com - pares.

D.S. al Coda
(with repeats)

COMPLICATED

Words and Music by AVRIL LAVIGNE, LAUREN CHRISTY,
SCOTT SPOCK and GRAHAM EDWARDS

Moderate Pop

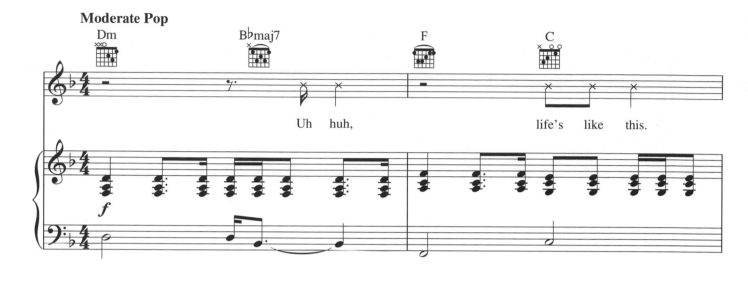

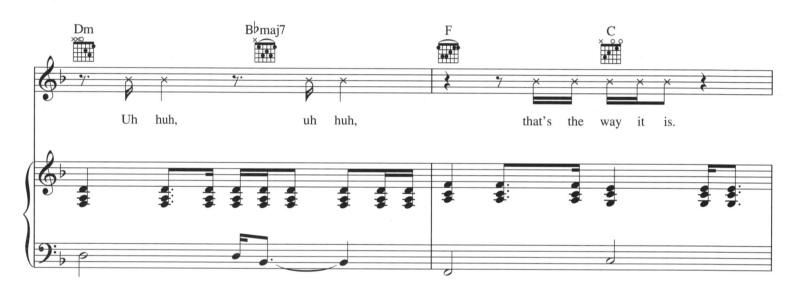

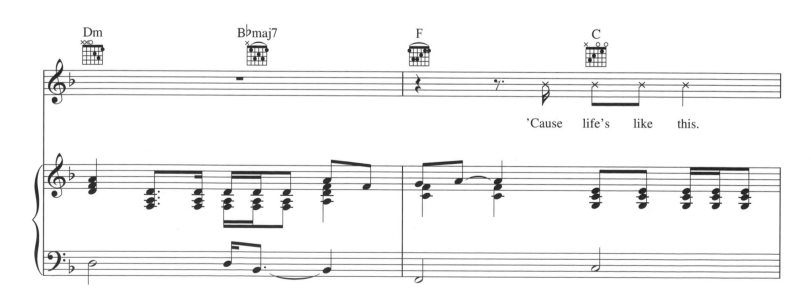

DON'T KNOW WHY

Words and Music by
JESSE HARRIS

DRIFT AWAY

Words and Music by
MENTOR WILLIAMS

G

You know ____ that's a game that I hate to
'Cause the world out - side looks so un -
and the rhythm ____ and rhyme looks and har - mo -

D   **Em**

lose.   I'm feel - in' the
kind.   Now I'm count - in' on
ny.   You help me a -

G   **To Coda ⊕**

strain;   ain't ____ it a shame? ____
you   to car - ry my through. ____
long,   mak - in' me strong. ____
                                                      Oh,

D   **A**

give me the beat, ____ boys, to soothe my soul; ____ I wan - na get lost in your

DRIVE

Words and Music by BRANDON BOYD,
MICHAEL EINZIGER, ALEX KATUNICH,
JOSE PASILLAS II and CHRIS KILMORE

EVERYDAY

Words and Music by JON BON JOVI,
RICHIE SAMBORA and ANDREAS CARLSSON

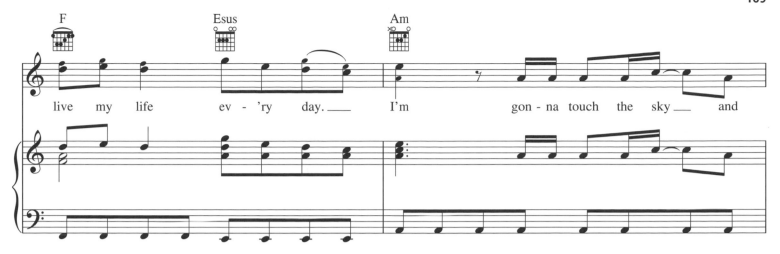

live my life ev-'ry day. ___ I'm gon-na touch the sky ___ and

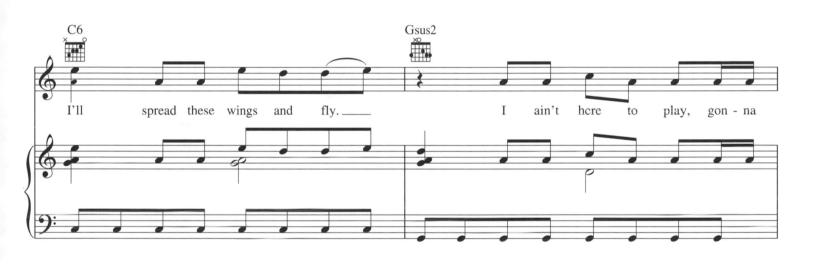

I'll spread these wings and fly. ___ I ain't here to play, gon-na

live my life ev-'ry day. ___ live my life ev-'ry day. ___

FALLEN

Words and Music by
SARAH McLACHLAN

Moderately slow

Heav-en, bend to take my hand and lead me through the fire. Be the
Heav-en, bend to take my hand, I've no-where left to turn. I'm

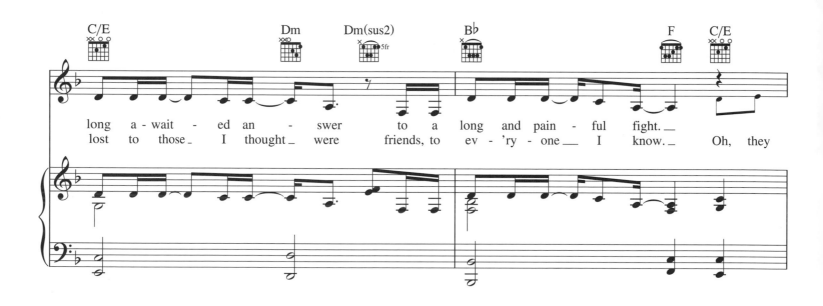

long a-wait-ed an-swer to a long and pain-ful fight.
lost to those I thought were friends, to ev-'ry-one I know. Oh, they

Truth be told, I've tried my best, but some-where a-long the way I
turn their heads, em-bar-rassed, pre-tend that they don't see, but it's

THE FIRST CUT IS THE DEEPEST

Words and Music by
CAT STEVENS

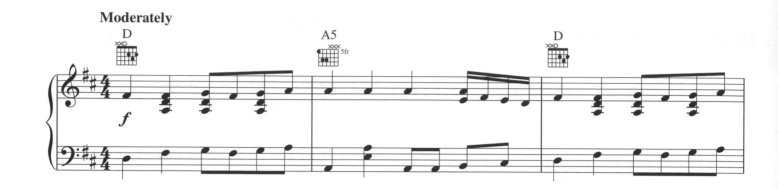

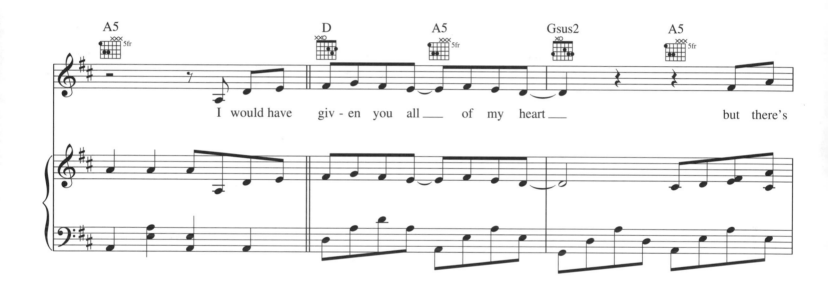

I would have giv-en you all ___ of my heart ___ but there's

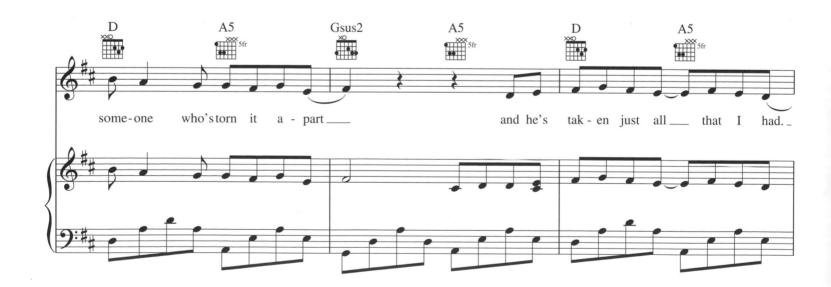

some-one who's torn it a-part ___ and he's tak-en just all ___ that I had. ___

FLYING WITHOUT WINGS

Words and Music by WAYNE HECTOR
and STEVE MAC

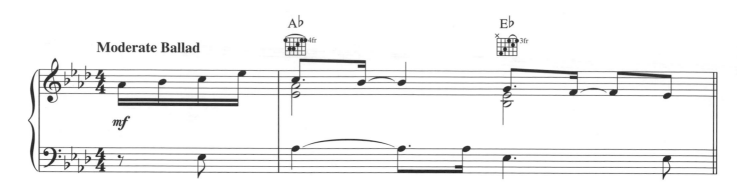

Ev-'ry-bod-y's look - ing for that some - thing.

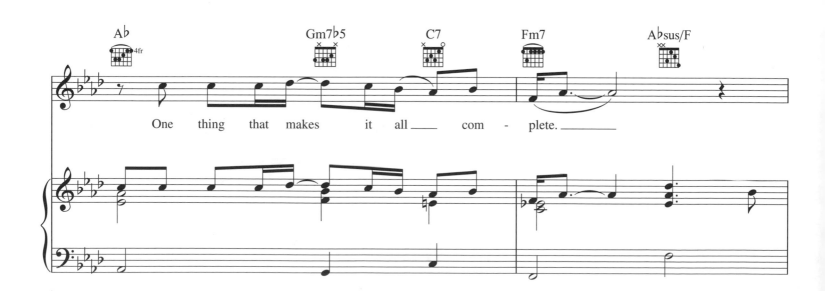

One thing that makes it all ___ com - plete. ___

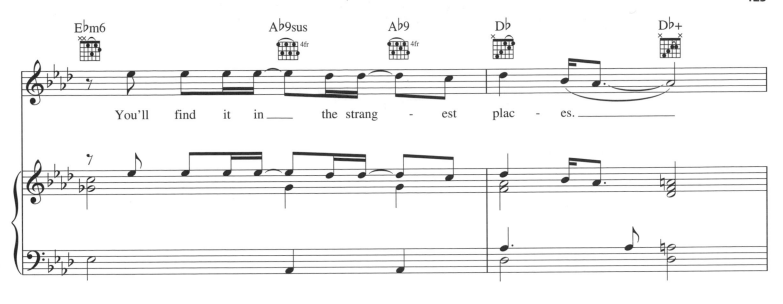

You'll find it in ___ the strang - est plac - es. ___

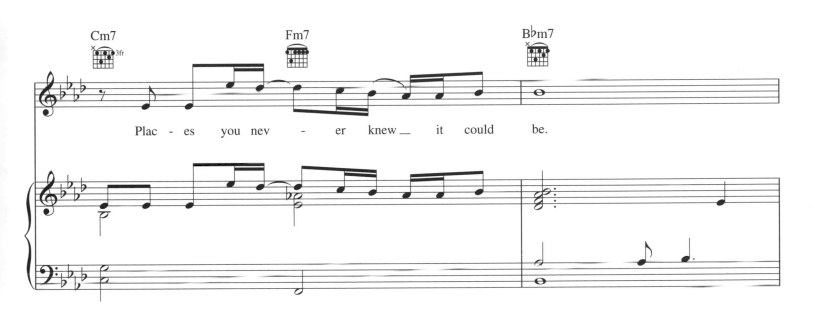

Plac - es you nev - er knew ___ it could be.

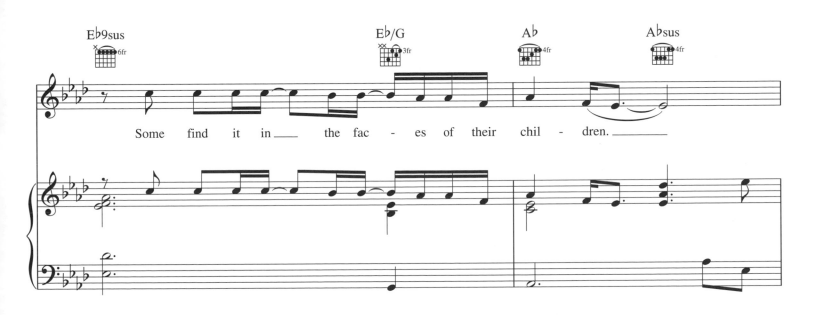

Some find it in ___ the fac - es of their chil - dren. ___

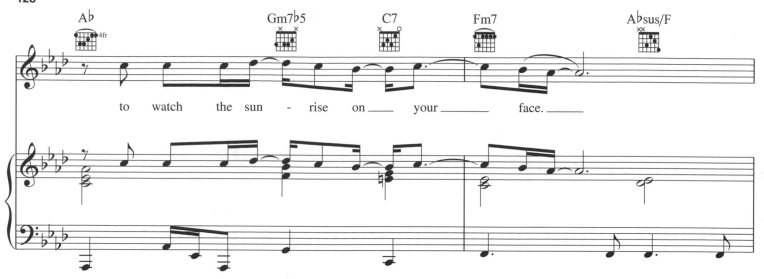

to watch the sun - rise on ___ your ___ face. ___

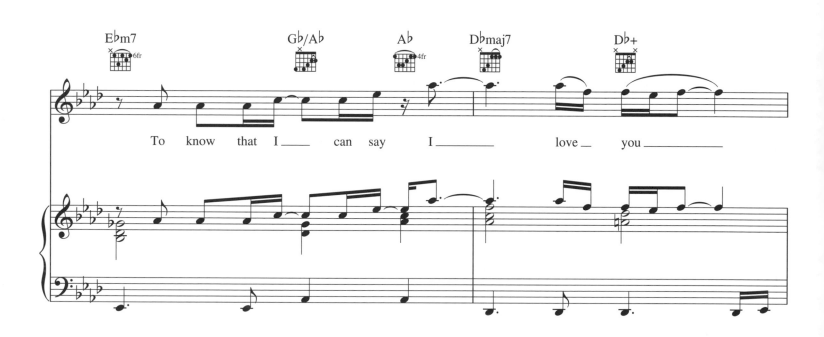

To know that I ___ can say I _____ love ___ you _____

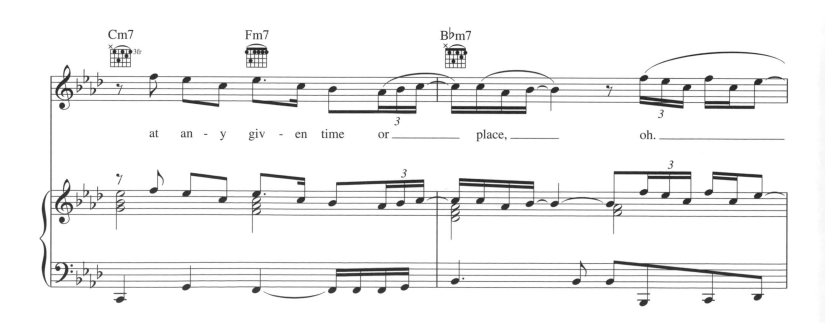

at an - y giv - en time or _____ place, _____ oh. _____

FREEDOM

Words and Music by
PAUL McCARTNEY

This is my right, ____

a right giv-en by God, ____ to live a free life, ____
who tries to take it a-way, ____ will have to an - swer, ____

to live in free - dom. ____ }
'cause this is my life. ____ }

Talk - ing a-bout

GET THE PARTY STARTED

Words and Music by
LINDA PERRY

* *Vocal written one octave higher than sung.*

HEAVEN

Words and Music by HENRY GARZA,
JOEY GARZA and RINGO GARZA

Save _____

Recorded a half step lower

heav - en? en?___ 'Cause I just got - ta know__ how far._____

I just wan - na know__ how far.____

Repeat and Fade

Guitar solo

Optional Ending

GIVE ME JUST ONE NIGHT
(Una Noche)

Words and Music by DEETAH,
ANDERS BAGGE and ARNTHOR BIRGISSON

Lips keep tell - ing me ___ you want ___ me ___

and hold me close ___ all through ___ the night. _____ And I know

give you the time of your life, _____ the time of your life. _____

_____ I'll give you the time of your

life. _____

To Coda

Your lust for pas-sion makes_ me cra-zy. _____

HELLA GOOD

Words and Music by PHARRELL WILLIAMS,
CHAD HUGO, GWEN STEFANI
and TONY KANAL

keep on danc - in'.

1

The per -

2

You got me

feel - in' hell - a good ___ so let's just keep on danc - in'. _____

You hold me like you should ___ so I'm gon - na

You got me feel - in' hell - a good __ so let's just

Keep on

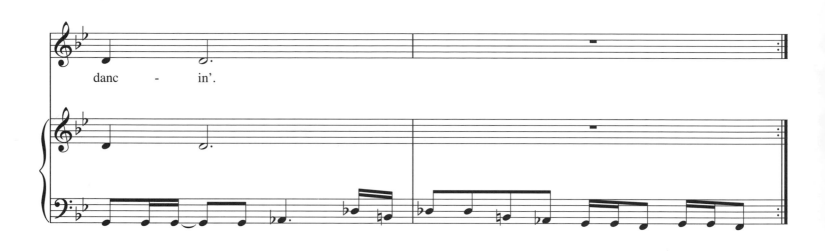

danc - in'.

HERE WITHOUT YOU

Words and Music by MATT ROBERTS, BRAD ARNOLD,
CHRISTOPHER HENDERSON and ROBERT HARRELL

Moderate Rock

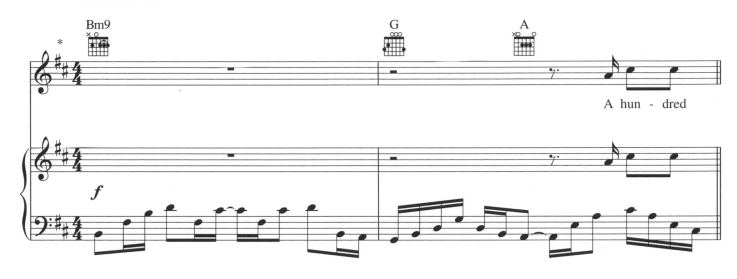

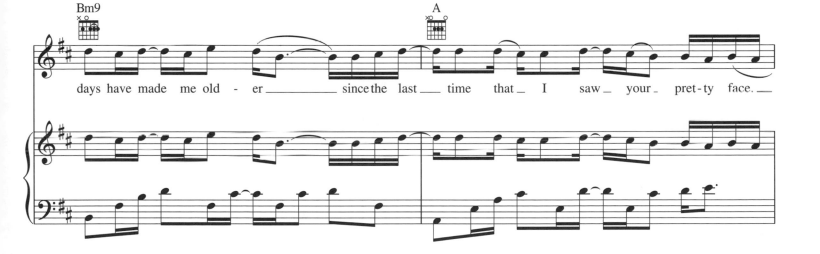

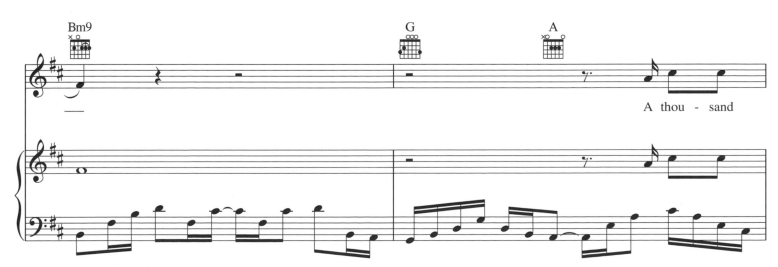

* Recorded a half step lower.

HEY YA!

Words and Music by
ANDRE BENJAMIN

Moderately

One, two, three, uhh. My ba-by don't mess a-round be-cause she

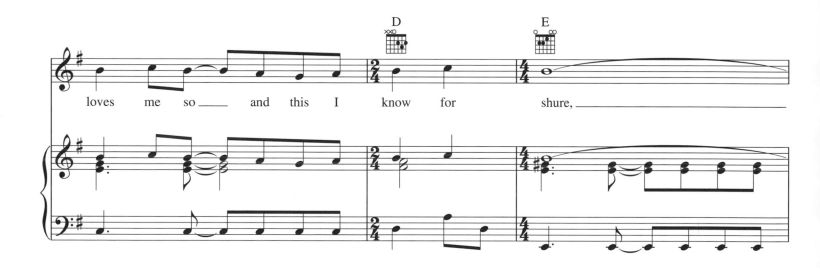

loves me so ___ and this I know for shure, ___

___ uhh. But does she real-ly want ___ to but can't

Rap 1: *(See additional lyrics)*

Shake it. Shake, shake it. Shake it. Shake it. Shake, it sug-ar.

Shake it like a Pol-a-roid pic-ture. Shake it. Shake it. Shake, shake it.

Rap 2: *(See additional lyrics)*

Shake it. Shake, shake it. Shake it. Shake it. Shake, shake it.

Shake it like a Pol-a-roid Hey _____ ya!

Additional Lyrics

Rap 1: (3000):   Hey, alright now. Alright now fellas!
(Fellas): Yeah!
(3000):   Now, what's cooler than being cool?
(Fellas): Ice Cold!!!!
(3000):   I can't hear ya. I say what's, what's cooler than being cool?
(Fellas): Ice Cold!!!!
(3000):   Alright, alright, alright, alright, alright, alright, alright, alright.
          Ok, now ladies.
(Ladies): Yeah!!!!
(3000):   Now, we gon' break this thing down in just a few seconds.
          Now, don't have me break this thing down for nothin'.
          Now, I wanna see y'all on y'all baddest behavior.
          Lend me some sugar, I am your neighbor, ahh. Here we go, uhh.

Rap 2:   Now, all Beyonces and Lucy Lius and Baby Dolls get on the floor.
          You know what to do. You know what to do. You know what to do.

I HOPE YOU DANCE

Words and Music by TIA SILLERS
and MARK D. SANDERS

hope you nev- er lose _____ your sense of won- der.
nev- er fear _____ those _____ moun- tains in the dis- tance.

I WANNA BE WITH YOU

Words and Music by KEITH THOMAS,
SHELLY PEIKEN and TIFFANY ARBUCKLE

I WANT LOVE

Words and Music by ELTON JOHN
and BERNIE TAUPIN

IF I'M NOT MADE FOR YOU
(If You're Not the One)

Words and Music by
DANIEL BEDINGFIELD

Slow Ballad

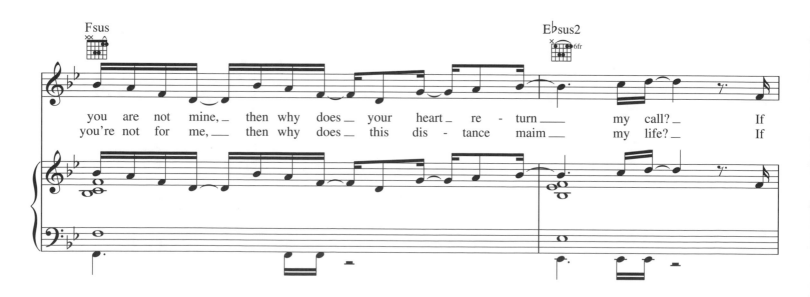

IN A LITTLE WHILE

Words and Music by MATTHEW SHAFER
and MICHAEL BRADFORD

Here's to the good life or so they say. All those par - ties and games that all those peo - ple play. They tell me this is the place to be. All these beau - ti - ful peo - ple and

On the oth - er side of a coin there's a face. There's a mem - o - ry some - where that I can't e - rase. And there's a place that I'll find some - day but some - times I feel like it's

D.S. al Coda

fin - 'ly __ see. __ I just won - der, won - der if you think a - bout me. _____

CODA

Yeah, _____ in a lit - tle while I'll be think - in' a - bout __ you. __

In a lit - tle while I'll still be ____ here with - out __ you. __ You nev - er gave me a rea -

- son to doubt __ you. __ In a lit - tle while I'll be think - in' a - bout __ you, ba -

INVISIBLE

Words and Music by DESMOND CHILD,
CHRISTOPHER BRAIDE and ANDREAS CARLSSON

JENNY FROM THE BLOCK

Words and Music by TROY OLIVER, ANDRE DEYO,
JENNIFER LOPEZ, JEAN CLAUDE OLIVIER,
SAMUEL BARNES, JOSE FERNANDO ARBEX MIRO,
LAWRENCE PARKER, SCOTT STERLING, M. OLIVER,
DAVID STYLES and JASON PHILLIPS

Moderate Hip Hop

Chil - dren grow and wom - en pro - duc - ing. Men go work - ing, some go steal - ing.

Ev - 'ry - one's got to make _ a liv - ing. L. O. X., yeah.

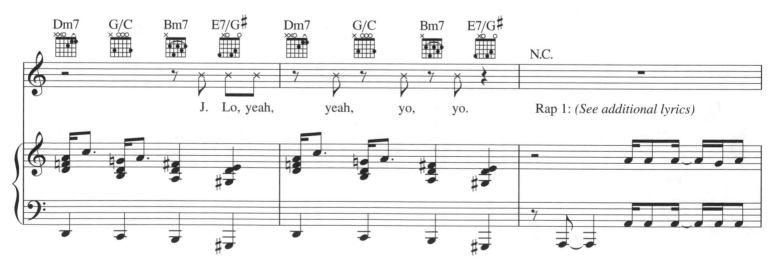

J. Lo, yeah, yeah, yo, yo. Rap 1: *(See additional lyrics)*

fooled by the rocks that I got. I'm still, I'm still Jen - ny from the block. Used to have a

lit - tle, now I have a lot. No mat - ter where I go I know where I came from, _ from the Bronx.
I'm down to

earth like this. Rock - in' this bus - 'ness. I've grown up so much.

I'm in con - trol and lov - in' it. Rum - ors got me laugh - in', kid. I

Additional Lyrics

Rap 1: We off the blocks this year.
Went from a 'lil to a lot this year.
Everybody mad at the rocks that I wear.
I know where I'm goin' and I know where I'm from.
You hear LOX in the air.
Yeah we at the airport out.
D-block from the block where everybody air forced out.
Wit' a new white tee you fresh. Nothin' phony wit' us.
Make the money, get the mansion, bring the homies wit' us.

Rap 2: Yo, it take hard work to cash checks
So don't be fooled by the rocks that I got, they're assets.
You get back what you put out.
Even if you take the good route, can't count the hood out.
After a while you'll know who to blend wit'.
Just keep it real wit' the ones you came in wit'.
Best thing to do is stay low, LOX and J. Lo.
They act like they don't, but they know.

LADY MARMALADE

Words and Music by BOB CREWE
and KENNY NOLAN

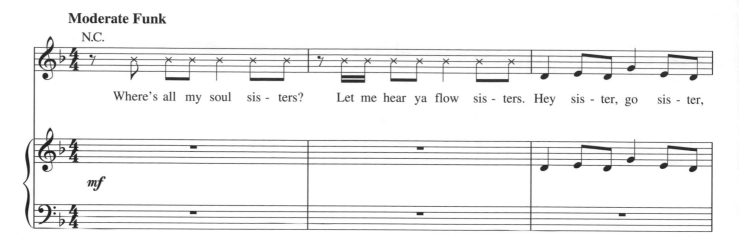

LUCKY

Words and Music by ALEXANDER KRONLUND,
MARTIN SANDBERG and RAMI YACOUB

(Spoken:) This is a story about a girl named Lucky.

Ear - ly morn-ing, she wakes up.

Knock, knock, knock on the door. It's time for make-up,

CODA

A♭sus   F   B♭m

lone - ly ___ heart, think - ing, if there's noth - ing

D♭/A♭   A♭/G♭   G♭   A♭sus   N.C.

miss - ing in my life, then why ___ do ___ these tears ___ come at night?

(Spoken:)... "Best actress, and the winner is...Lucky!"

"I'm Roger Johnson for Pop News standing outside the arena waiting for Lucky. Oh my God, here she comes!"

"She's so luck-y, she's a star." But she cry, cry, cries in her

lone - ly_____ heart, think - ing, if there's noth - ing

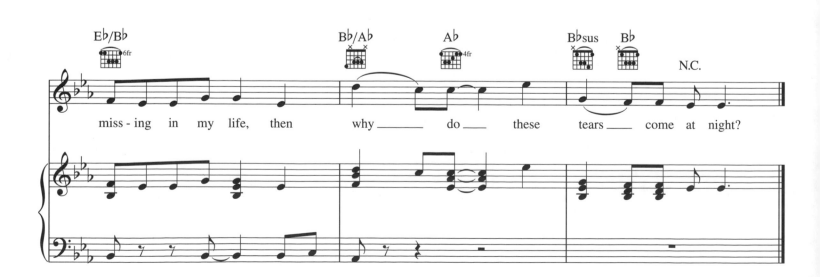

miss - ing in my life, then why_____ do_____ these tears_____ come at night?

MEANT TO LIVE

Words and Music by JONATHAN FOREMAN
and TIM FOREMAN

Hop - ing that he's bent for more _ than ar - gu - ments _ and failed at - tempts _ to fly, _____ fly. _____ We were meant _ to live _ for so _ much more. _ _____ Have we lost _ our - selves? _ Some - where we live in - side, _____

A MOMENT LIKE THIS

Words and Music by JOHN REID
and JORGEN KJELL ELOFSSON

Recorded a half step lower.

Some peo-ple search _ for-ev-er for that one spe-cial kiss. _

Oh, I can't be-lieve _ it's hap - pen-ing _ to me. _____ Some

peo - ple wait _ a life-time for a mo-ment _ like this. _

Choir: (Mo-ment like this.) ___
Lead vocal ad lib.

1985

Words and Music by MITCH ALLEN,
JOHN ALLEN and JARET REDDICK

Driving Rock

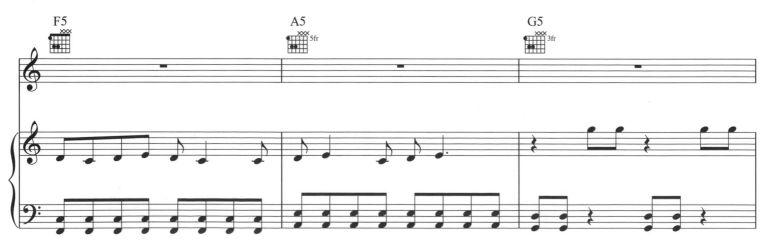

* Recorded a half step lower.

SHE WILL BE LOVED

Words and Music by ADAM LEVINE
and JAMES VALENTINE

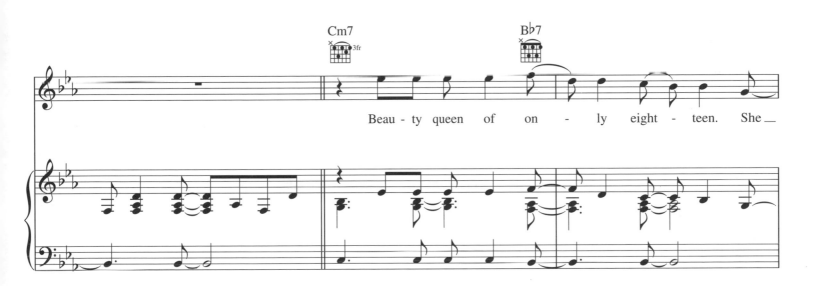

ON THE WAY DOWN

Words and Music by RYAN CABRERA,
CURT FRASCA and SABELLE BREER

100 YEARS

Words and Music by
JOHN ONDRASIK

Moderately fast

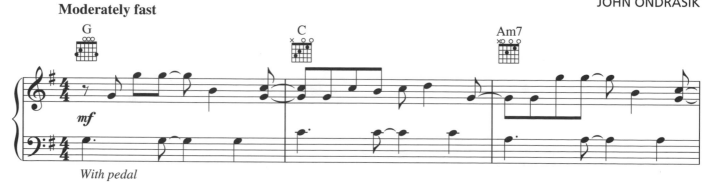

mf

With pedal

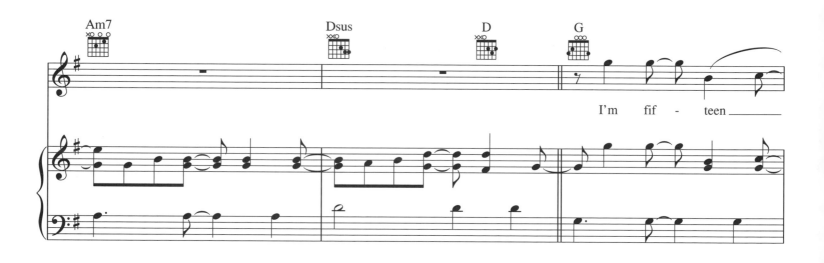

I'm fif - teen _____

_____ for a mo - ment,   caught in _____ be - tween _____ ten and twen - ty and I'm _____

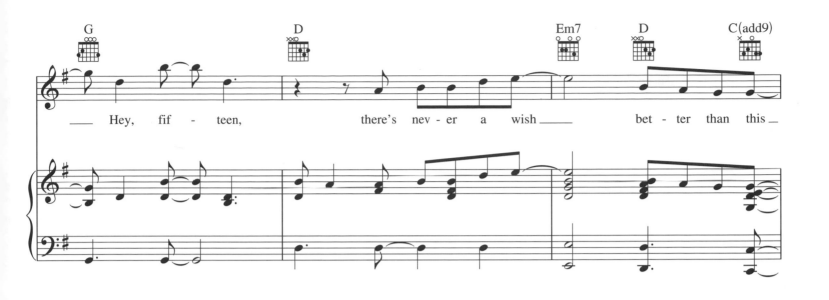

Hey, fif - teen, there's nev - er a wish _____ bet - ter than this _____

_____ when you on - ly got _____ a hun - dred years to live. _____

OUT OF MY HEART
(Into Your Head)

Words and Music by ANTHONY GRIFFITHS,
CHRISTOPHER GRIFFITHS, CHRISTIAN BURNS,
MARK BARRY and STEPHEN McNALLY

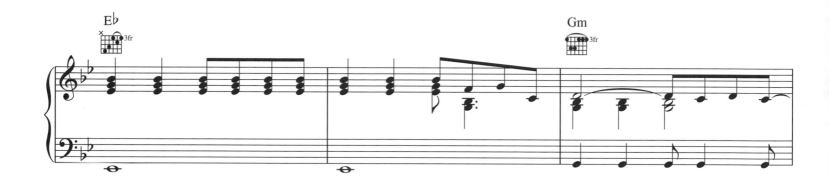

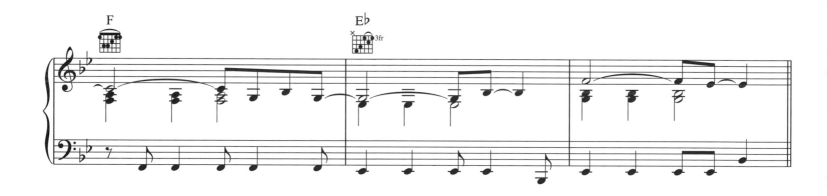

Lyrics:
I feel ___ fine. ___
Chas-ing the sun. ___

Now the rain ___ is gone ___ and the sun ___
Try'n to get ___ a - way ___ from the rain ___

RAIN ON ME

Words and Music by BURT BACHARACH,
HAL DAVID, ANDRE PARKER,
IRVING LORENZO and ASHANTI DOUGLAS

Slow groove

I'm look-in' in the mir-ror at this wom-
See, I don't wan-na hug my pil-low late

-an down and out. She's in-ter-nal-ly dy-ing and knew this is not
at night no more. I'm toss-in' and turn-in' and think-in' 'bout burn-

what love's a-bout. I don't want to be this wom-an the
-in' down these walls. I don't want to fuel this fire no

* Recorded a half step lower.

ROCK THE BOAT

Words and Music by STEPHEN GARRETT,
RAPTURE STEWART and ERIC SEATS

Moderately slow groove

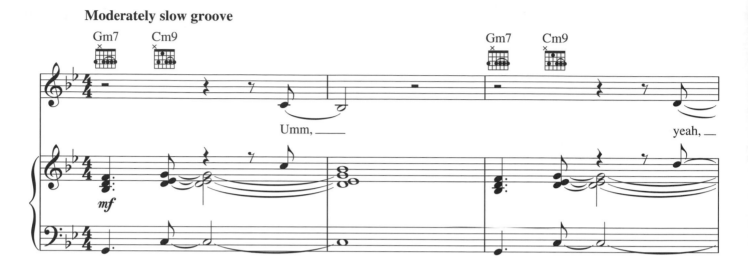

Umm, _____ yeah, _____

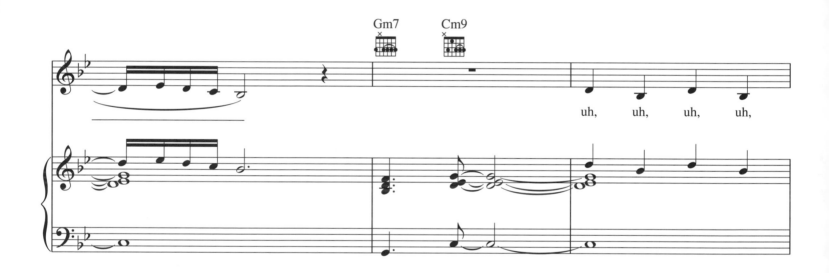

uh, uh, uh, uh,

umm __ umm, umm, __ yeah! Boy you know you make me

Gm7 Cm9
close.
Ba - by let's take this o - ver-board now. I want _ you to
Gm7 Cm9 Gm7 Cm9
rock. the boat. Work it in the mid - dle.
(Rock the boat. Rock the boat. Rock the boat. Rock the boat. (Work the mid - dle.
Gm7 Cm9
Change po - si - tions. Now
Work the mid - dle. Work the mid - dle.) (New po - si - tions. New po - si - tions. New po - si - tions.)
Gm7 Cm9 Gm7/B♭ E♭maj7 F/G Gm7 Cm9
stroke it ba - by. Stroke it for me. Stroke it for _ me. Stroke it for _ me. Ooh _ ba - by, I love your

SHE BANGS

Words and Music by DESMOND CHILD,
WALTER AFANASIEFF and ROBI ROSA

Medium fast Latin

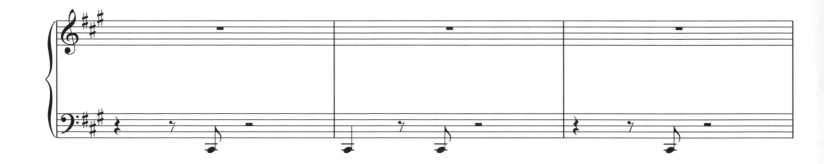

CODA

Instrumental solo

And if La - dy Luck __ gets on my side __ we're gon - na

SO YESTERDAY

Words and Music by GRAHAM EDWARDS,
SCOTT SPOCK, LAUREN CHRISTY
and CHARLIE MIDNIGHT

Moderate Rock

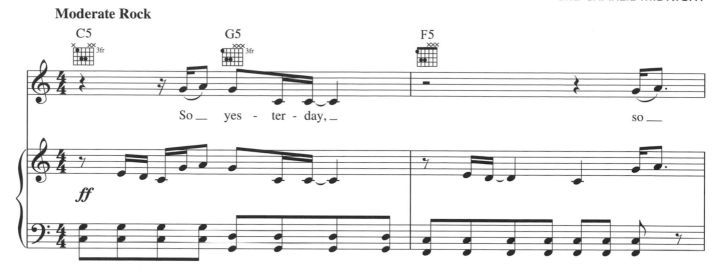

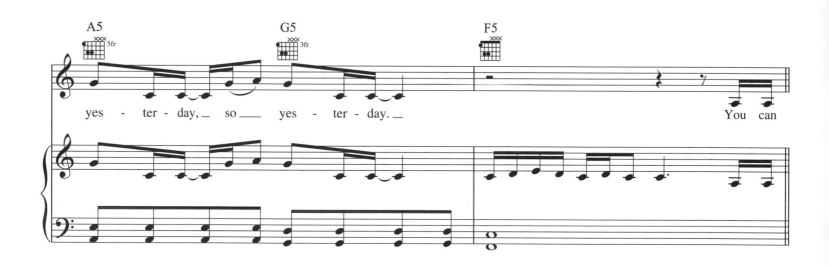

So __ yes - ter - day, __ so __

yes - ter - day, __ so __ yes - ter - day. __ You can

change your __ life if you wan - na. You can change your __ clothes if you wan - na. If you
say you're __ bored if you wan - na. You could act real __ tough if you wan - na. You could

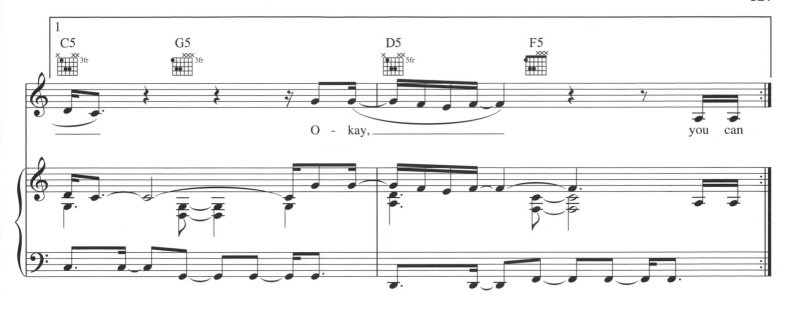

1

C5   G5   D5   F5

O - kay, _____ you can

2

C5   G

_____ If you're o - ver me, I'm al - read - y o - ver you. _

Fmaj7   G

___ If it's all been done,_ what is left to do?___ How can you hang up___ if the line is dead?_

SOMEWHERE OUT THERE

Words and Music by RAINE MAIDA,
JEREMY TAGGART and DUNCAN COUTTS

Last time I talked to you, you were lonely and out of place.
Down here in the atmosphere, garbage and city lights.

You were lookin' down on me, lost out in space.
You've gone to save your tired soul. You've gone to save our lives.

* *Recorded a half step lower.*

TAKE MY BREATH AWAY
(Love Theme)
from the Paramount Picture TOP GUN

Words and Music by GIORGIO MORODER
and TOM WHITLOCK

THE SPACE BETWEEN

Words and Music by DAVID J. MATTHEWS
and GLEN BALLARD

Additional Lyrics

2. The rain that falls splashed in your heart,
   Ran like sadness down the window into your room.

3. The space between our wicked lies is where
   We hope to keep safe from pain.

4. Take my hand 'cause
   We're walking out of here.

5. Oh, right out of here.
   Love is all we need, dear.

THANK YOU

Words and Music by PAUL HERMAN
and DIDO ARMSTRONG

Vocal written one octave higher than sung.

Original key: G# minor. This edition has been transposed up one half-step to be more playable.

Push the door; I'm home at last, and I'm soak - ing through and through.

THERE YOU'LL BE

Words and Music by
DIANE WARREN

THIS LOVE

Words and Music by ADAM LEVINE
and JESSE CARMICHAEL

I'll fix ___ these bro - ken things. ___

Re - pair ___ your bro - ken wings ___ and make ___ sure ev - 'ry - thing's ___ al -

- right. ___ It's al - right. ___ My pres - sure on ___ your hips. ___

Sink - ing ___ my fin - ger - tips to ev - 'ry inch ___ of you ___ be - cause I know ___

A THOUSAND MILES

Words and Music by
VANESSA CARLTON

Mak-ing my way down-town, walk-ing fast. Fac-es pass and I'm home-bound.

Recorded a half step higher.

UNDERNEATH YOUR CLOTHES

Words and Music by SHAKIRA
Music co-written by LESTER A. MENDEZ

WASTING MY TIME

Words and Music by DANNY CRAIG,
DALLAS SMITH, JEREMY HORA
and DAVE BENEDICT

WHEREVER YOU WILL GO

Words and Music by AARON KAMIN
and ALEX BAND

YOU RAISE ME UP

Words and Music by BRENDAN GRAHAM
and ROLF LOVLAND

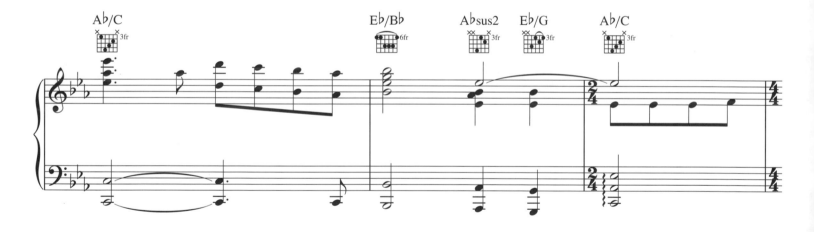

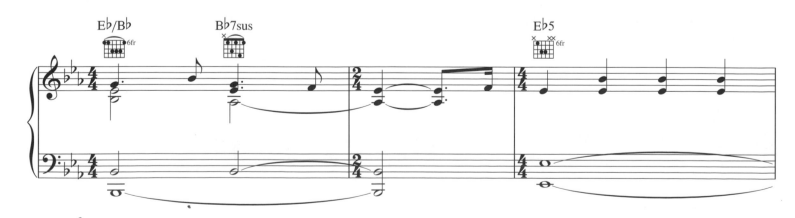

WHO LET THE DOGS OUT

Words and Music by
ANSLEM DOUGLAS

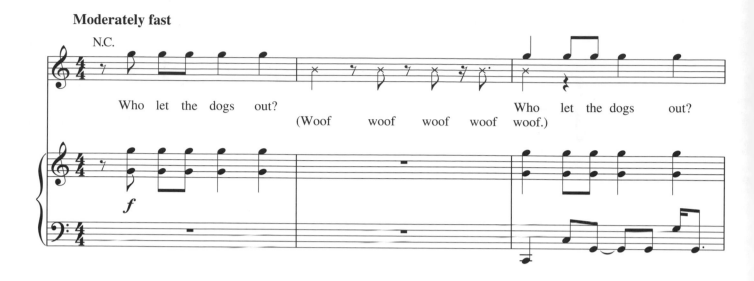

Additional Lyrics

Well if I am a dog, the party is on.
I gotta get my groove on 'cause my mind done gone.
Do you see the ray comin' from my eye,
Walkin' through the place like Digi-man
Just breakin' it down.
Me and my white silk shorts I can't see color.
Any color will do. I'll stick on you,
That's why they call me pit bull.
'Cause I'm a man of the land;
When they see me they say ooh.